WHAT PEOPLE ARE SAYING ABOUT *NOT EVEN A HINT* BY JOSHUA HARRIS

"This is a timely book. Josh boldly deals with the strongest attacks on young men and women today. It's hard to be God's man or God's woman when we continually feel and experience the failures of our sinful nature. This book is a practical call to personal holiness. I am happy to endorse such an endeavor."

CHRIS TOMLIN
SIXSTEP RECORDS ARTIST/WORSHIPER

"Full of wise, practical insight, this book offers help and hope—not just for those who are dealing with sexual lust, but for anyone besieged by temptation or battling besetting sins of any kind."

NANCY LEIGH DEMOSS, AUTHOR AND HOST OF THE
REVIVE OUR HEARTS RADIO PROGRAM

"We cannot waste time playing hide-and-seek with lust and its consequences. Joshua Harris has earned our trust by talking straight and teaching from the Word of God. His wisdom on the true nature of lust will not only inform but challenge every Christian."

R. ALBERT MOHLER JR., PRESIDENT,
SOUTHERN BAPTIST THEOLOGICAL SEMINARY

"I am very encouraged that my longtime friend Josh Harris has written a book about lust, speaking about the place where compromise begins—the mind. May God use this book to keep many from allowing their minds to become 'the devil's playground.'"

REBECCA ST. JAMES, SINGER/SONGWRITER

"The main issue with lust is that it hinders us from seeing and savoring the glory of Christ. That hurts us and dishonors Him. So, for your joy and Christ's honor, I commend this book to you. It is realistic, practical, and hope-giving because of uncompromising grace. The pure in heart will see God. If you want that sight, let Josh Harris help you fight."

JOHN PIPER, PASTOR OF
BETHLEHEM BAPTIST CHURCH, MINNEAPOLIS

"I may not have kissed dating goodbye, but *Not Even a Hint* is one of the most powerful books I've read. Josh writes honestly and transparently, giving practical counsel on fighting lust. This is an absolute must-read for anyone who is serious about living righteously."

JERAMY CLARK, AUTHOR OF *I GAVE DATING A CHANCE*

"Joshua Harris has done it again. You hold in your hand undiluted biblical truth on a vital topic, served up with honesty and humility. I'm not aware of another book quite like it."

C. J. MAHANEY, AUTHOR OF
THE CROSS CENTERED LIFE

"Wow! This book is guts and grace intertwined. *Not Even a Hint* is a work of colossal importance for both guys and girls. Our generation is in desperate need of this message."

ERIC AND LESLIE LUDY, AUTHORS OF
WHEN GOD WRITES YOUR LOVE STORY

"A beautiful blend of grace and truth. My friend Joshua Harris raises high standards of holiness while carefully avoiding legalism. Honest, biblical, and practical—I highly recommend it."

RANDY ALCORN, BESTSELLING AUTHOR OF
THE TREASURE PRINCIPLE AND *THE PURITY PRINCIPLE*

"Forthright, honest, and compelling. Joshua Harris has written a book about sexual purity that can be read and applied by both men and women. He shows us in practical and specific ways how we can grow toward God's standard—absolute purity in mind and body."

JERRY BRIDGES, AUTHOR OF
THE PURSUIT OF HOLINESS

JOSHUA HARRIS

WITH BRIAN SMITH

A STUDY GUIDE  FOR

MEN

not *even* a hint

Multnomah® Publishers *Sisters, Oregon*

NOT EVEN A HINT: A STUDY GUIDE FOR MEN
published by Multnomah Publishers, Inc.

© 2004 by Joshua Harris
International Standard Book Number: 1-59052-253-2

Cover design by Steve Gardner/His Image Pixelworks
Cover image by PIER/Getty Images

Unless otherwise indicated, Scripture quotations are from:
The Holy Bible, New International Version
© 1973, 1984 by International Bible Society,
used by permission of Zondervan Publishing House

Other Scripture quotations are from:
The Holy Bible, English Standard Version (ESV)
© 2001 by Crossway Bibles, a division of Good News Publishers.
Used by permission. All rights reserved.

Multnomah is a trademark of Multnomah Publishers, Inc.,
and is registered in the U.S. Patent and Trademark Office.
The colophon is a trademark of Multnomah Publishers, Inc.

Printed in the United States of America

For information:
MULTNOMAH PUBLISHERS, INC.
POST OFFICE BOX 1720
SISTERS, OREGON 97759

04 05 06 07 08 09 10—10 9 8 7 6 5 4 3 2 1 0

CONTENTS

The reason Brian Smith's name graces the cover of this book is because it was his hard work that made it possible. After I wrote *Not Even a Hint*, Brian took the time to both create the format of this study guide and write the questions. As you'll see, he's done a terrific job. My role was to edit Brian's draft—I changed some questions, cut a few, and added others. But Brian did the majority of the work, and for that I'm very grateful.

Introduction

This study guide is designed for men who are serious about helping each other grow in holiness. It's designed to spark open, honest, and godly discussion about male sexuality. Sex isn't just something to joke about in the locker room—it's a beautiful and sacred gift from God. We want to be both thankful for it and respectful of God's commands to be pure. This study guide will challenge you to apply the principles of *Not Even a Hint* in your daily lives in order to guide you to victory in the ongoing battle against lust.

WHO CAN USE IT?

The *Not Even a Hint Study Guide for Men* is extremely versatile. It can be used in a group setting or individually. However, it is designed primarily for two or more men who want to work through the book together. Whether this is a group of three friends that meets weekly at a coffee shop or fifteen guys in a Sunday school class, the guide can be adapted to meet your needs.

There are different ways for a group to use it. One option is for each member to have his own copy of the study guide and work through the appropriate lesson on his own before each meeting, writing his answers and then coming to the meeting ready to share. (This is ideal, since it encourages each guy to think through answers more carefully.)

The second option is for only the leader to have a copy of the study guide. With this approach, group members read the appropriate chapter in *Not Even a Hint* before the meeting, and then the leader uses the study guide at the meeting to lead discussion. If you use this approach, make sure you encourage group members to do some of the self-examination exercises suggested throughout the book on their own time.

WHAT'S IN EACH LESSON?

There is one lesson for each of the ten chapters in *Not Even a Hint*. Each lesson contains the following elements to help you dig deeper into the message and apply its truth:

EASY REVIEW

At the beginning of each lesson we've listed the *central issues,* or main points, of the corresponding chapter in *Not Even a Hint (NEAH)*. This summary is a great way to quickly refresh your memory about the essence of the chapter. We've also listed a few *key growth objectives* for you so you'll understand what we hope you will know, feel, and do after working through the lesson.

QUESTIONS

The first couple of questions in each lesson are meant to be *discussion starters,* to provide a nonthreatening way to get people talking. Have fun with them.

Most of the remaining questions are either *conceptual* questions, inviting you to deal with ideas or concepts in the book; or *application* questions, guiding you toward putting the concepts into practice in your life. (Many of the questions are preceded by a quote from *Not Even a Hint* to remind you of important principles and to help direct the focus of your discussion.)

ACCOUNTABILITY FOLLOW-UP

Near the end of each lesson are two *accountability follow-up* questions, usually relating to the main issues of the preceding lesson. Don't end the meeting until you've checked in on each other's progress in a truthful and caring manner.

MEDITATE AND MEMORIZE

We also list a key Scripture passage, which we encourage you to write out on a card and carry with you during the week. Only when you hide God's Word in your heart will His truth be readily available so that His Spirit can help you gain victory over lust. Ideas for meditating on and memorizing these passages are provided in *NEAH* (158) and in lesson 9 of this study guide.

CUSTOM-TAILORED ACTION PLAN

If this study is to help you experience true freedom and victory over sexual temptation, you have to come away with a specific plan of action, and that plan must be tailored uniquely to you. There is no "one size fits all" solution for lust. Every guy's collection of battlefields, strengths, and weaknesses is unique to him.

Beginning with chapter 4 and continuing through chapter 10, you will be guided, step by step, through the formulation of a Custom-Tailored Action Plan using a simple worksheet on pages 68–71 of the study guide. Your plan is completely flexible—you can revise it whenever and however you wish. And it is designed so that you can easily photocopy it for accountability partners.

HOW TO LEAD A GROUP DISCUSSION ON LUST

Regardless of the size of the group, it's helpful to have one member serve as the leader. He's the one who is responsible to assign the appropriate chapter for the group to read before each meeting, to ask the questions, and to facilitate discussion. If no one else steps up to that role, we encourage you to simply start leading. You don't need a label…just do the job, and the group will function more smoothly and effectively.

Of course, the topic you're tackling is unique. In order to help each other feel safe about sharing honestly, we urge you to take these guidelines seriously:

1. PROMISE AND MAINTAIN CONFIDENTIALITY

In the very first meeting, agree that nothing shared in the group will leave the group without the sharer's permission. (The rare and only exception is information you might need to divulge in order to protect a group member or someone else from harm. If you think this might be the case, seek a pastor's guidance.)

2. CREATE AN ATMOSPHERE OF TRUTHFUL ACCEPTANCE

Each of us is capable of the darkest of sins, and each of us is fighting a hard battle. Group members should listen to one another with compassion and acceptance. This does not mean sacrificing truth, but rather listening with understanding and "speaking the truth in love" (Ephesians 4:15).

3. BE AN EXAMPLE OF HUMBLE HONESTY

Whether you are the designated group leader or not, you can serve the group by stepping out and sharing honestly about your sin and your victories. As friendships and trust develop, you'll encourage others to overcome their fears about sharing by overcoming yours first.

MORE TIPS FOR LEADING A GROUP

1. STRIVE FOR APPLICATION

James 1:22 says, "Do not merely listen to the word, and so deceive yourselves. Do what it says." Remind the guys in your group that merely reading a book—even the Bible—and talking about it won't produce change. Real change occurs after we close the book and do something about it. As you progress through the study guide, take time during your meetings to have guys share what changes they've made.

2. START SMALL

While application is important, no one can change in every area all at once. Encourage members of your group to begin by trying to apply just one point from each chapter.

3. OUTLAW ONE-WORD ANSWERS

The questions in the *NEAH Study Guide for Men* are intended to provoke discussion and even debate. Ban yes and no answers. Encourage guys in your group to share from their heart, not just parrot the "right" answer from *Not Even a Hint*. Giving only expected or "acceptable" answers will not help them examine their own lives.

4. LISTEN TO THE HOLY SPIRIT

This study guide exists to serve *you*—don't become a slave to it. If one question opens up a fruitful discussion, then go with it! Don't feel you have to work through all of the questions. Take opportunities for the group to pray spontaneously for someone who expresses a need. Let God's Spirit, not this book's format, guide you.

5. ENCOURAGE, ENCOURAGE, ENCOURAGE!

Point out to your friends when you see them growing in a certain area—no matter how small it is. The best way to motivate each other is to acknowledge where God is at work. Offer lots of encouragement.

6. FOCUS ON GOD

In the midst of focusing on the challenge of lust, make sure that the group's primary motive is to please and honor God. Keep reminding each other of the gospel—Christ's death and resurrection has set us free from the rule of sin! We're forgiven! Begin and end your time with prayer. Enjoy the journey! Remember, only God's Spirit can work real change in our lives. May God use your study and interaction to bring about life-changing results.

Not Even a Hint

Why Can't I Seem to Beat Lust?

Now that you've read chapter 1 of *Not Even a Hint,* we hope you realize that you're not alone. Almost everyone experiences frustration when dealing with lust. The enemy would like you to believe that you're isolated and unusual, but you're not. And you can find safety among carefully chosen brothers in Christ who are willing to honestly face their sin and together pursue holiness.

God offers real hope through the victory of Jesus Christ. Begin your study with a simple prayer expressing your trust in His death and resurrection. Thank Him for giving you the desire to change.

CENTRAL ISSUES

- Lust defined: craving sexually what God has forbidden.
- There are right and wrong *standards* for holiness, *power sources* for change, and *motives* for fighting sin.
- We're not just against lust; we're *for* God's good plan for sex in marriage.

KEY GROWTH OBJECTIVES

✓ To establish that lust is something we all face in some form.
✓ To understand why God's standard is "not even a hint" of impurity in our lives.
✓ To realize that killing lust leads to the joy and freedom of holiness.

1. Honestly, how realistic does the standard *not even a hint* seem to you with regard to sexual sin? Why did you choose this response?

    1   2   3   4   5   6   7   8   9   10
    Are you crazy?   We can do it!

2. Whether you think this is a realistic standard or not, rate how strongly you *desire* to have not even a hint of sexual sin in your life. Why?

1   2   3   4   5   6   7   8   9   10
Forget it!   I can't wait!

LUST VERSUS SEXUALITY

In *Not Even a Hint,* Josh writes, "I have a simple definition for lust: craving sexually what God has forbidden" (*NEAH* 18).

3. What is helpful to you in Josh's definition? What would you change in the definition, if anything? Why?

4. **Part of the challenge Christians face in a lust-filled world is remembering that neither sex nor sexuality is our enemy. Lust is our enemy and has hijacked sexuality. We need to keep reminding ourselves that our goal is to rescue our sexuality from lust so we can experience it the way God intended** (*NEAH* 26).

Summarize from the following Scripture passages God's thinking about the differences between lust and pure sexuality (see also *NEAH* 25–28).

Lust—Ephesians 5:3; Colossians 3:5; 1 Thessalonians 4:3–4

Sexuality—Genesis 2:22–25; Proverbs 5:18–19; 1 Corinthians 7:2–5

5. God never calls us to sacrifice as an end in itself, but only *through* sacrifice on the way to great joy. On the other side of the seeming loss and denial is always reward and pleasure so deep and so intense that it's almost impossible to call what you gave up a sacrifice at all (*NEAH* 27).

If this is true, then describe what is really happening…

…when you give in to lust.

…when you resist lust.

6. What is an example of you (or someone you know) passing up the instant pleasure offered by lust for a deeper, more lasting pleasure later? What sacrifice do you think God is calling you *through* for the sake of true joy and godly pleasure?

OUR EFFORTS VERSUS GOD'S PROVISION

7. At the beginning of chapter 1, Josh describes his futile efforts to live up to "the contract":

The year that followed was a very humbling lesson in how utterly incapable I was of being righteous in my own strength…. All my great ambitions, all my vows, all my self-efforts were revealed to be worthless (*NEAH* 18).

Describe a time when you tried to accomplish something good on your own when you actually needed outside help.

8. God's standard of *not even a hint* quickly brings me to the end of my own ability and effort. It reminds me that God's standard is so much higher than the standards I place for myself that only the victory of Christ's death and resurrection can provide the right power and the right motive needed to change me (*NEAH* 25).

Why was each element of God's plan better than Josh's original plan (see *NEAH* 22–25)?

	GOD'S PLAN	JOSH'S PLAN
Standard of holiness	*not even a hint*	*no masturbating for a year*
Power source for holiness	*the cross of Christ*	*his own willpower*
Motivation for holiness	*God's grace*	*to show God that he was good*

FORGIVENESS VERSUS CONDEMNATION

In the preface, Josh writes, "I've learned that I can only fight lust in the confidence of my total forgiveness before God because of Jesus' death for me" (*NEAH* 10). If you have put your faith in Christ as your Savior, are you confident of your total forgiveness before God? Do you believe He loves and accepts you because of Jesus' sacrifice for you? Without this confidence, it will be difficult to be honest about lust in your life with other carefully selected Christian brothers.

9. Summarize the central point of each of these statements from God to you:
1 Timothy 1:15–16

Psalm 103:8–13

1 Corinthians 10:13

1 John 1:6–9

10. Honesty with others takes courage. Take a minute to talk with God the Father about any fear you have about discussing the topic of lust. Ask His Holy Spirit for courage and a deep hunger for holiness.

ACCOUNTABILITY FOLLOW-UP

Starting with lesson 2, this section will guide your group to review commitments or action points from preceding lessons in order to evaluate your progress and to encourage you toward greater obedience in God's strength. In this first lesson (especially if you're with a group of guys you don't know well), use the following questions to begin your journey.

11. What is one question you would like us to ask you on a regular basis?

12. What is one way you want us to pray for you this week in keeping with this lesson? (Write down each other's requests and take a few minutes to pray for each other.)

MEDITATE AND MEMORIZE

> *But among you there must not be*
> *even a hint of sexual immorality,*
> *or of any kind of impurity, or of greed,*
> *because these are improper for God's holy people.*
> EPHESIANS 5:3

What God Called Good

Is It Biology or Is It Sin?

CENTRAL ISSUES

- God has built into men and women a strong sexual desire, which is pure and good.
- Shame is appropriate when we sin, but misplaced shame distracts us from the real enemy.
- Lust comes out of evil desires in our own hearts and constitutes active rejection of God.
- We must express both gratitude for our sexuality and restraint over lust

KEY GROWTH OBJECTIVES

- ✓ To express gratitude for your sexuality.
- ✓ To soberly acknowledge the dangers of lust.
- ✓ To learn to distinguish between pure sexuality and lust.

Some people reject God-given sexuality as dirty. Others accept indiscriminate sexual indulgence as normal. As you've learned while reading *Not Even a Hint* chapter 2, either extreme is misleading and dangerous. God designed us to embrace our sexuality while resisting lust.

We can't carry out this balancing act without God's help. Stop now and ask Him for discernment, that you might understand clearly what He says in His Word and that you might see the difference between godly sexuality and sinful lust in your own experience.

1. Describe one or two ways you've gotten the wrong message that sex in itself is bad or that lust is okay.

2. Why do you think these misconceptions are so widely accepted?

SEXUALITY IS GOOD

In *Not Even a Hint,* Josh writes:

> Our sex drive is in some mysterious way part and parcel of our drive to build, advance, conquer, and survive. Our sexuality and our sex drive are intertwined and tied together with our creativity and with our innate human desire to continue life on this spinning planet. Being a sexual being with sexual desires is part of what it means to be a human created in God's image. (*NEAH* 34)

3. What does each of the following passages say or assume about your sexuality (see also *NEAH* 33–36)?
   Genesis 1:27–28; 9:7

   Genesis 2:22–25

   Song of Songs 2:3–4; 4:10 (about a married couple)

4. When we break God's commands, shame is appropriate.... [But] misplaced shame can be dangerous because it saps our strength for fighting our real enemy. A person who is wrongly ashamed of being a sexual creature with sexual desires will quickly feel overwhelmed and helpless because he's trying to overcome more than just lust—he's trying to stop being human! (*NEAH* 36–37).

What do you honestly think of your God-given sexuality most of the time (see also *NEAH* 36–38)?

LUST IS BAD

While rejecting your sexuality is definitely not God's plan, the opposite error of indulging your every desire *is* sinful (see also *NEAH* 38–41).

5. Why is it important to remember the source of lust (James 1:13–14; Matthew 15:18–19)?

6. Why is it important to remember that sexual sin offends God (1 Thessalonians 4:7–8; Psalm 51:4–5)?

7. **God says *not even a hint* because you can't give in to lust's demands and hope to pacify it. It always grows. And as it does, lust will rob you of your ability to enjoy true, godly pleasure. You can't bargain with lust and come out a winner** (*NEAH 41*).

What do victory and fulfillment look like, according to God? *Ephesians 4:19–24*

Philippians 1:9–11

8. **Though lust longs for an object or a person, ultimately this object is not its prize; its goal is the very *act* of desiring. The result is that lust can never be quenched. As soon as the object of lust is attained, lust wants something more** (*NEAH 41*).

REAL LIFE: You're helping your Christian friend Ethan move, and in one box you see a stack of men's magazines. You ask Ethan about them, and he nonchalantly says, "Hey, buddy, you know how it is. You and I both have our needs that we gotta take care of, right? It's not like I'm sleeping with anyone."

How will you respond to him? Consider Ephesians 4:19. Where is the "line" he is drawing for himself? How likely is he to hold that line?

SO WHAT'S THE DIFFERENCE?

As Christians, embracing our sexuality looks radically different. We don't obey every sexual impulse—nor do we deny that we have sexual desires. Instead we choose both restraint and gratefulness (*NEAH* 42).

9. Think of a sexual impulse or temptation you experienced during the last week or two, and write out what you might have prayed in that moment. Express to God both your gratitude for your sexuality and your desire to resist temptation (see Josh's sample prayers on pages 37–38 of *NEAH*).

10. This week, practice responding to sexual impulses by going to God in prayer. (In the next lesson you'll be prompted to look back and reflect on how it went.) Take a moment now and ask the Holy Spirit to help you remember throughout the week the grace and power to obey that He always offers you.

ACCOUNTABILITY FOLLOW-UP

Use these or similar questions to support and encourage each other, or for individual self-evaluation before God.

11. How did you do this past week at...
    ...*accepting God's* standard *for holiness (not even a hint)?*

    ...*drawing on God's* power source *for holiness (the cross of Christ)?*

    ...*having the right* motive *in your pursuit of holiness (God's grace)?*

12. How, specifically, can we pray for you or otherwise encourage you?

MEDITATE AND MEMORIZE

When tempted, no one should say,
"God is tempting me." For God cannot be tempted by evil,
nor does he tempt anyone; but each one is tempted when,
by his own evil desire, he is dragged away and enticed.
JAMES 1:13–14

You Can't Save Yourself

Where Can I Find the Power to Change?

G et ready, guys. Because you've read *Not Even a Hint* chapter 3, you already know that this lesson is going to challenge your natural tendency to do things—even good things—your own way. But self-reliant effort won't cut it. God alone provides the means for victory.

Take a moment and ask God to grant you humility to rely on Him for victory and to accept *His* best for your life, rather than what might seem best to you.

1. In *Not Even a Hint,* Josh writes, "Here's what you have to remember: You need to be rescued. You need God's grace" (*NEAH* 49). How does this compare with what you've been taught by your family, by the media, in school, in church?

CENTRAL ISSUES

- Legalistic self-sufficiency cannot save us; rather, we are sanctified in God's power *because* He has already justified us.
- The gospel is our *power source* for holiness and freedom, and grace is our *motivation.*
- Both legalism and sinful indulgence enslave us; the Holy Spirit can lead us to a life of freedom.

KEY GROWTH OBJECTIVES

✓ To recognize your inability to save yourself.
✓ To understand how justification *empowers* us and grace *motivates* us to be holy.
✓ To learn to rely on the Holy Spirit's power and to avoid both legalism and indulgence.

2. What honestly comes to mind when you hear the word *holiness*? Why?

YOU'RE NEVER ON YOUR OWN

It's normal for people to want to do things their own way, in their own strength, but...

> ...rules and regulations that stem from self-righteous and self-centered motivations can actually take us away from God. John Owen taught that trying to put our sin and lust to death based on our own human strength is the "essence and substance of all false religion in the world." Even a good guideline for fighting lust, if it's "carried out with man-made schemes, always ends in self-righteousness" (*NEAH* 48).
>
> Legalism is trying to add to what Jesus did when He died and rose again. Legalism is seeking to relate to God based on our work, instead of based on the work of our representative and mediator, Jesus Christ (*NEAH 49–50*).

3. Why is it futile to try in our own strength to achieve salvation (Romans 3:20), or obedience and spiritual growth after salvation (Galatians 3:3)? (See also *NEAH 47–50*.)

4. How does the good news of Jesus' death and resurrection give us *power* for holy living?
   Romans 6:5–8

   Romans 8:1–4

5. How does God's grace provide us with *motivation* to resist temptation?
    Titus 2:11–14

.   *Hebrews 4:15–16*

TRUE FREEDOM, GOD'S WAY

In *Not Even a Hint* (51–52), Josh takes great care to distinguish between our justification and our sanctification.

6. From these Scripture passages, summarize what happens when you are *justified*:
    Romans 3:22–26

    Romans 10:9–10

    Titus 3:3–7

    By the way, if you're not certain whether you have received God's forgiveness and been justified in His sight, we encourage you to talk to a pastor or other Christian leader so that you can be sure.

7. Now read these passages, and describe the process of *sanctification* (the word means "being made holy") in the life of a Christian:
    1 Thessalonians 4:3–5

    1 Thessalonians 5:23–24

8. All the necessary and important aspects of pursuing holiness don't add to our salvation; they're the *response* to and the *result of* God's finished work of justifying us. Christ died so that we could be freed from the hopeless task of trying to justify ourselves (*NEAH* 52).

Don't doubt your forgiveness. When you feel condemned and separated from God, you're more likely to turn back to lust for comfort, and that's certainly not what God wants you to do. Don't let anything distract you from the rock-solid reality that when God forgives, you're truly forgiven (*NEAH* 53–54).

If these statements are true, then what *are* the right motives for a Christian's pursuit of sanctification (spiritual growth and victory over sin)?

9. The gospel frees us to do what we were originally created to do: enjoy and glorify God with our whole lives. The gospel sets us free to be holy (*NEAH* 55).

Think of your own life and heart. Describe how holiness manifests itself as freedom for you (see Galatians 5:13–14; Romans 6:16–19; also *NEAH* 54–55).

THE GUIDE FOR LIFE'S PATH

The only way we can hope to live a life of holy freedom is under the guidance of God's Holy Spirit (see *NEAH* 55–58).

10. Describe the kinds of freedom God's Holy Spirit can provide when we follow Him.
    Romans 8:5–6

    Romans 8:26–27

    Galatians 5:16–25

11. Picture the Spirit-guided life as a proven but narrow path winding between two deep ravines. The safe path of grace and Christian freedom travels between the treacherous pits of legalism on one side and indulgence in sin on the other. For centuries, misguided people have twisted Scripture to justify leaving the path of freedom for one or the other.

    In a similar way, this book you're holding could be misused. One person could apply its practical examples and advice for putting sin to death in a legalistic manner. Another person could take its emphasis on grace and forgiveness as an excuse to indulge in sin (*NEAH* 57–58).

Choose one Scripture passage or one scriptural principle (stated in your own words) that will help you avoid both legalism and indulgence as you complete this series of lessons. Write it down; then stop and invite the Holy Spirit to help you retain this truth in your heart and mind.

ACCOUNTABILITY FOLLOW-UP

12. How did you do during this last week, turning to God in prayer about your sexual impulses? How did you affirm to Him the goodness of your sexuality, as well as the dangers in the temptations you face?

13. What difference, if any, did these cries for help make in your ability to resist temptation?

MEDITATE AND MEMORIZE

You, my brothers, were called to be free.
But do not use your freedom to indulge the sinful nature;
rather, serve one another in love.
GALATIANS 5:13

A Custom-Tailored Plan

Where Am I Weakest, and What Can I Do?

CENTRAL ISSUES

- Each man's vulnerabilities to temptation are unique to him.
- Every man needs to think through the various times, places, and sources that contribute most strongly to his sexual temptation.
- We each need to establish a specific, customized plan, focusing on one battle at a time.

KEY GROWTH OBJECTIVES

✓ To acknowledge your uniqueness in the battle against sexual temptation.
✓ To help you assess your unique vulnerabilities.
✓ To begin designing a practical plan for dealing with sexual temptation in your life.

I t's tempting to think that just *reading* chapter 4 in *Not Even a Hint* is sufficient to help you resist lust. But ideas aren't enough—you need a specific plan of action. And you need God's wisdom. Ask Him now to give you courage to look honestly at yourself and to plan for decisive action.

1. In *Not Even a Hint,* Josh says, "Lust is kept alive and our weaknesses are fortified by the small provisions we give it" (*NEAH* 65). He describes radical actions people have taken to avoid small concessions to lust— canceling Internet service, choosing video rentals through the store window, paying for an unused gym

membership. How does this honestly feel to you? Overly zealous? Wise? Something else? Why do you say this?

YOU'RE ONE OF A KIND

God has designed you with unique strengths and personality traits. In similar fashion, you also have your own vulnerabilities (see *NEAH* 62–64).

> Each of us is unique in how we're tempted to lust.... This is why there can be no "one size fits all" approach to combating lust. That's also the reason it would be a mistake to evaluate how you're doing in this area by comparing yourself to others. It's possible to think you're "above lust" just because you're not struggling with it like someone else you know (*NEAH* 62–63).

2. How willing are you to take an honest look at your weaknesses, without comparing yourself to anyone else?

   1   2   3   4   5   6   7   8   9   10
   I can't handle it   I'm an open book

   Why do you think you chose this response?

3. What might help you increase your openness to self-examination by one or two points? (Do you have any concerns about your study group that could be set at ease? Consider praying Psalm 139:23–24.)

WHERE ARE YOUR DEFENSES WEAK?

> My bigger outbreaks of sin are usually triggered by smaller
> sins that I wasn't diligent in guarding against. I'm talking
> about the daily, even hourly decisions of what to watch,
> read, listen to, and allow my mind to think about and my
> eyes to rest upon (*NEAH* 64–65).

4. Read Romans 13:14. How far should you take "make no provision
   for the flesh" if you're truly "put[ting] on the Lord Jesus Christ"
   (ESV)? (Think about the example of Jesus' life [Hebrews 4:14–15].)

5. A lot of people can admit that lust is a prevalent sin in their life
   and say they want to change. But...they've never taken the time
   to think through how the process of temptation unfolds for them.
   Instead of anticipating and being on their guard, they're
   surprised by the same attack over and over (*NEAH* 62).

Let's take stock. But first, stop briefly and invite the Holy Spirit to
help you deal with any resistance you might have so you will be open to
His guidance.

a. List a few *times* of the day, week, or year that present difficult sexual
   temptation for you (see *NEAH* 65–66).

b. List a few *locations* that you need to avoid, or where you need to
   limit your time (see *NEAH* 66–67).

c. Describe any *sources* of sexual temptation that you find difficult to
   resist (see *NEAH* 67–74).

START YOUR CUSTOM-TAILORED PLAN

Your life will not change until you take action—specific and dramatic action—on what you know, drawing constantly upon God's strength and wisdom. Starting with this lesson, and continuing through lesson 10, we will guide you through the completion of a Custom-Tailored Action Plan for dealing with your unique vulnerabilities to lust (see pages 68–71 of this study guide). It is important to remember that the information you write in your Action Plan is totally flexible and can be updated or adjusted as necessary.

6. The truth is that we can't deal with everything at once. That's why my advice is to pick one area to begin working on. Choose a specific item from your list to make your focus. Take it to God in prayer. Repent of your apathy toward sin and determine what obedience would look like.

    Then seek to be faithful in that area. Take it seriously. Pray about it. Fight the little battles. Flee temptation. As God gives you grace to change in that area, you can move on to another area (*NEAH* 77–78).

    Go back over your responses to question 5, praying for wisdom to choose the most strategic lust triggers to address first. Mark one *time* under question a, one *location* under question b, and no more than three *sources* under question c. Transfer these selected items to steps 6 through 8 of your Action Plan (page 69 of this study guide).

7. Ask the Holy Spirit for wisdom, and complete step 9 of your Action Plan, choosing only one lust trigger for focused battle over the next few weeks.

8. Once you have made your selection, turn again to God and thank Him in advance for the victory He has promised. Embrace God's command to fix your eyes on Jesus "so that you will not grow weary and lose heart" (Hebrews 12:3).

ACCOUNTABILITY FOLLOW-UP

9. Did you recognize God's help this last week as you sought to travel the middle road, avoiding both legalism and sinful indulgence? What happened?

10. What is one way we can support you and pray for you to help you avoid these opposite errors?

MEDITATE AND MEMORIZE

But put on the Lord Jesus Christ,
and make no provision for the flesh,
to gratify its desires.
ROMANS 13:14, ESV

Guys and Girls

How Are We Different, and How Can We Help Each Other?

I n this fallen world, it's not normal for anyone to put the needs of others before himself. But God's grace in our lives makes supernatural conduct the norm. The Holy Spirit can help us see women as our sisters, rather than as objects.

Take a moment and ask Him to give you an attitude that supports rather than undermines women in their battle with lust. (And be sure you've read *Not Even a Hint* chapter 5 before starting this lesson.)

1. Cindy, a twenty-year-old single, writes:

> "A lot of times I think that a girl's struggle with lust is more emotional than a guy's. Of course I can only speak from personal experience but I think that in general girls are more creative and our imaginations can run away with us. It's difficult to guard your thoughts and fantasies about being in

CENTRAL ISSUES

- Both men and women battle lust, and all lust is sinful.
- Men and women are "wired" differently sexually, in ways that beautifully complement each other.
- Guys must understand the ways women are sexually tempted, and help their female friends not to stumble sexually.

KEY GROWTH OBJECTIVES

✓ To correct stereotypes and understand the real differences between men and women.
✓ To understand the *generally* typical sexual pitfalls of men and women.
✓ To learn to speak and behave around women in such a way as to minimize their sexual temptation.

a relationship or being married and all that goes along with that. For me it doesn't necessarily start out with this raging desire for sex but a longing to be held and loved that can become lustful."

Is it easy or hard for you to take seriously Cindy's battle with lust? Why?

THE TRUTH ABOUT GUYS AND GIRLS

The world is full of deception and misconceptions about the sexual makeup of women and men. And this misinformation keeps us from knowing how to fight the real battles.

2. Isn't it wonderful how God has made men and women to interact with each other? He made men visually oriented, then made women beautiful. He made men initiators, and then designed women to enjoy being pursued.... All this is part of God's wonderful design (*NEAH* 85).

In your own words, describe what is good about God's design for male and female sexuality (see *NEAH* 84–85).

3. In the section "Are All Men Monsters?" (*NEAH* 82–84), Josh writes:

The truth is that men's lust is more obvious, but not necessarily more sinful. Guys are typically more visually oriented, and as a result their lust is more visible. And because God made men to initiate and pursue women, their expressions of lust are often more aggressive and blatant.... Is a guy's lust, which is blatant and obvious, worse than a girl's lust, which is more refined and subtle? (*NEAH* 82–83).

How would you answer Josh's question? How does this help you understand the inner workings of your female friends? Or yourself?

4. In case we guys might use the seriousness of a girl's struggle with lust as an excuse not to take our own lust seriously, Josh writes:

> The point is that *all lust is bad.* Apart from God's grace
> working in us and changing us, we're all monsters.
> Regardless of how lust is expressed, it's motivated by a sinful
> desire for the forbidden. Lust is always based on the same
> lie—that satisfaction will be found apart from God (*NEAH* 84).

What is one step you will take in order to invite the help of God and your male friends as you deal with temptation? (This might be the same as step 9 of your Action Plan.)

HOW GIRLS ARE TEMPTED

> Lust blurs and bends true masculinity and femininity in harmful
> ways. It makes a man's good desire to pursue all about
> "capturing" and "using," and a woman's good desire to be
> beautiful all about "seduction" and "manipulation." In general it
> seems that men and women are tempted by lust in two unique
> ways: men are tempted by the *pleasure* lust offers, while
> women are tempted by the *power* lust promises (*NEAH* 85–86).

5. Describe one way that giving in to your temptation might make a girl's battle with temptation even harder (see *NEAH* 85–88).

6. Since women are especially lured by the prospect of a relationship, why do Christian guys need to consider carefully how they speak and act around their female friends?

7. In our efforts to protect our sisters in Christ, we might be tempted to "shun them in love" in an attempt to avoid any danger of leading them on. But this can be hurtful. Describe a healthy balance for a brother's behavior and speech toward his sister in Christ.

8. REAL LIFE: You've noticed that at church group activities your friend Chad has established a pattern of choosing one girl or another and giving her special attention, gazing into her eyes and offering flattering compliments. On the way to your cars one evening, you mention it to him. He says, "Hey, I'm just having fun. Besides, the girls eat it up. Can't you see them melting right there in front of me?"

How will you respond? (What seems to be Chad's attitude toward his sisters? What desires might he be trying to satisfy through his behavior?)

HELPING YOUR FEMALE FRIENDS

Our membership in God's family must transform our view of the opposite sex. We're not trying to get something from each other: we're called to give, to love, and to care for one another. The opposite sex shouldn't be viewed as a bunch of potential partners—they are men and women created in God's image, whom Christ died to save. They're family! (*NEAH* 94).

9. With what motives and attitudes does God want you to relate to
   your female friends?
   1 John 3:16

   Romans 14:13

   2 Timothy 2:22

10. Read back over *NEAH* pages 86–87, 89–90. Brainstorm a few ways
    you might help your female friends through...
    ...the clothes you wear.

    *...the ways you interact physically with them (hugs, other touching, body
    language).*

    *...the things you say to them (such as hinting at an intimate relation-
    ship).*

11. From your ideas in question 10, choose one or two, and transfer
    them to step 18 of your Custom-Tailored Action Plan on page 71 of
    this study guide. Take a minute and ask the Holy Spirit to help you
    put your commitment into practice.

ACCOUNTABILITY FOLLOW-UP

12. How did you do this week dealing with your chosen "lust trigger" (see step 9 of your Action Plan)? How did the Holy Spirit help? Other people (accountability partners)?

13. How can we continue to encourage and support you?

MEDITATE AND MEMORIZE

No temptation has overtaken you that is not common to man.
God is faithful, and he will not let you be tempted beyond your ability,
but with the temptation he will also provide the way of escape,
that you may be able to endure it.
1 CORINTHIANS 10:13, ESV

Self-Centered Sex

How Do I Deal with Masturbation?

Talking about masturbation is embarrassing. No doubt about it. But as you read in *Not Even a Hint* chapter 6, masturbation is a common struggle, and talking it over with guys who understand can help us not only achieve victory, but also remember that the reason this issue matters is because we want to love and honor God.

So why not ask God now to help you lay down any pride and get the support and perspective you need in order to love Him first and fully in heart and in action?

1. Besides locker-room jokes, have you ever talked about masturbation with someone else?

- The issue of masturbation should not be the defining focus of our spirituality—God is more concerned with the soil of our hearts, out of which this act grows.
- The reason masturbation is often tied to lust and reinforces a self-centered view of sex.
- You can take several practical steps to keep from masturbating and to find restoration after failing.

KEY GROWTH OBJECTIVES

✓ To help you think through your own convictions regarding masturbation and God's purpose for sex.
✓ To establish a specific plan to keep from masturbating and to find forgiveness and the power of God's grace after lapses.

2. As you were growing up, what were the standards of your parents or other authority figures regarding masturbation?

CENTERING YOUR HEART ON GOD

As in any area of our lives, God must be at the center of our sexuality (*NEAH* 99–101).

> I think Christians make too big a deal of masturbation in that we obsess over the act and neglect the more important issues of the heart.... God wants us to be more concerned with the soil of our hearts, out of which a lifestyle of masturbation grows. It's a mistake to make the act of masturbation the measure of our relationship with God (*NEAH* 99).

3. What does God want from you more than anything else (Deuteronomy 6:5; Matthew 22:37–40)? What might this look like as you grow in holiness over the next ten years?

4. God's solution for our guilt is not to change His definition of sin. God dealt with our guilt at the cross of Christ (*NEAH 100*).

How does God deal with sexual sin in your life?
1 Peter 3:18

Romans 6:3–7

5. Lust is a serious sin. Masturbation is one expression of a lustful heart. But when we inflate the importance of this act, we'll either

overlook the many evidences of God's work in us or we'll ignore other more serious expressions of lust that God wants us to address (*NEAH* 100–101).

For just a moment, set aside the issue of masturbation. List at least…
…*one area in which you're growing.*

…*one other important area of growth that needs your attention.*

Throughout the rest of this lesson, try to keep your focus on loving and pleasing God, rather than on fear and shame. Stop now and ask the Holy Spirit to help you rest in His grace.

IS MASTURBATION RIGHT OR WRONG?

6. Look back over *NEAH* pages 101–103 and 106, and write a response to each of the following arguments. Use Scripture passages to support your responses whenever possible.

● Argument #1: *Masturbation is a natural, physiological act—it doesn't affect the spiritual* (consider Galatians 5:22–24).

● Argument #2: *I can masturbate without lusting* (consider Jeremiah 17:9).

● Argument #3: *I need masturbation while I'm single; when I'm married, it won't be a problem* (consider 2 Peter 2:19b).

7. First...sex belongs to God. He created our sexuality and is the
   only One with the authority to dictate how it should be
   expressed. Sex is for Him. All that we do as sexual creatures
   should be an expression of our honor, love, and fear of Him.
       Second, a God-centered view of sex strives to honor
   God's purpose for sex. It's not enough to know God's *rules*
   for sex. We need to understand his purpose and plan for it
   (*NEAH* 104).

   What does each of the following passages say about God's purpose
   and plan for sex (see also *NEAH* 103–106)?
   Proverbs 5:15–23

   1 Corinthians 7:3–5

   Hebrews 13:4

8. How does God's view of sex affect your conviction about
   masturbation (see *NEAH* 106–108)?

PLANNING AHEAD

9. REAL LIFE: One night before you fall asleep you start to replay
   sexual images and fantasies in your mind. You're convicted that you
   should stop, but you feel your body responding to your lustful
   thoughts. You tell yourself, *If I masturbate and take care of it, then I
   can move on and the temptation will be over.*

Is this thinking true? What safeguards do you wish you had in place? Who among your male Christian friends comes to mind as being able to provide support for you?

10. God is after your heart. That's what He cares about. He wants your undivided passion. As your mind is renewed by His Word and as you put away wrong thinking, lust's power will steadily weaken in your life. Set realistic expectations. Complete change will take time and effort (*NEAH* 110).

With a view toward giving God your fully devoted heart, list several practical ways to stop masturbating (see *NEAH* 108–112).

11. If you fail and give in to temptation, what is the best way to love and please God from that moment on?
    Hebrews 4:14–16

    1 John 1:9

12. From your ideas in question 9, choose one or two, and transfer them to step 10 in your Custom-Tailored Action Plan. Take a moment and ask God to give you awareness of His grace, which empowers you to obey.

ACCOUNTABILITY FOLLOW-UP

13. How have you been doing in the battle to deal with your chosen "lust trigger"? (See step 9 of your Action Plan.)

14. Have you done anything differently lately to make the battle against lust easier for any of your female friends? (See step 18 of your Action Plan.) Tell us about it.

MEDITATE AND MEMORIZE

Love the LORD your God with all your heart
and with all your soul and with all your strength.
DEUTERONOMY 6:5

Half a Poison Pill Won't Kill You

How Do I Cope with the Temptations of Media?

I t's possible that this lesson will require the greatest courage to tackle because it touches on a part of your life where you may never have considered making a sacrifice. The media's influence is so subtle that the danger is sometimes hard to take seriously. But as you read in chapter 7 of *Not Even a Hint*, the little choices add up.

Ask God right now to change your assumptions and values where He sees the need, even though it may not be obvious to you.

1. What do you honestly think of Mrs. Wesley's description of sin in *NEAH* (120)? How is it helpful? What would you change?

CENTRAL ISSUES

- The media can be subtly dangerous because it bypasses reason and goes straight for our affections.
- We must confront our tendencies to justify harmful content and begin to evaluate our entertainment according to godly standards.
- Discernment is more than disapproval—it's *taking action* to change our habits.

KEY GROWTH OBJECTIVES

✓ To become alert to the subtle dangers of the media.
✓ To learn to practice biblical discernment in entertainment choices.
✓ To choose one or two specific steps of action.

MEDIA—FRIEND OR FOE?

Nearly all of us grew up with the virtual reality of the entertainment world. That's why the influence of the media can take us by surprise. It helped shape us during our formative years and has been a persistent part of our life experience. Let's do our best to step back and see it for what it really is (see also *NEAH* 115–119).

2. Time for a little quick math—based on an average day, figure out how many hours of TV and/or movies you watch per week, per month, per year. Are you surprised by the amount of time? Do you feel good about it?

3. Television and film stir up feelings and emotions that bypass our minds and go straight for our affections. The incredible power of media is that it can make something evil look good or exciting without appearing to make any argument at all! (*NEAH* 118).

    Describe an instance when a movie or TV show gripped you emotionally—for good or for harm. What does this say about the sheer power of the media?

4. There's probably not a more important little battle than the daily decisions we make in the area of movies and television (*NEAH* 116).
    We need to examine the cumulative effect of our media habits on our attitude toward God, toward sin, and toward

the world.... They can slowly and subtly undermine biblical truth and conviction in our hearts (*NEAH* 119).

Choose one popular TV show, and try to identify the "small" messages it conveys about such topics as authority, responsibility, integrity, honesty, men and women, sex, God, or any other important issues. Does this show have a positive or negative influence on Christian viewers?

EXERCISING DISCERNMENT

It doesn't matter what something is rated, or how popular it is, or how seemingly innocent it appears. If it hardens your heart toward God, if it obscures your awareness of the ugliness of sin and the holiness of God, if it takes the edge off your spiritual hunger, then it's sin (*NEAH* 120).

5. Summarize how each of these passages can help guide our media selections.
   1 Thessalonians 5:21–22

   Ephesians 5:1–4

   Ephesians 5:8–12

   Psalm 101:2–4

6. Choose one movie you've seen recently. With that movie in mind, answer each of the following questions. Briefly explain each answer.

- *Does the movie or television show increase the strength and authority of your body over your mind (NEAH 120)?*

- *Does it make sin seem attractive to you (NEAH 121)?*

- *Can you honestly thank God for the entire portrayal (NEAH 121)?*

- *Does it promote an evil message or use an evil method (NEAH 123)?*

7. As you work through these questions, you may want to yell "legalism!" But remember, legalism has to do more with the *motive* with which you apply a moral standard than with the standard itself (see lesson 3 and *NEAH* chapter 3). How can these kinds of standards for media selection be compatible with God's grace (consider Galatians 5:13 and Titus 2:11–12)?

TAKING ACTION

We seem to think that because we don't approve [of a movie or show]…we can watch all the garbage in the world and our souls won't be affected. We call this "discernment." But that's as foolish as saying that if you don't enjoy a calorie, it won't make you fat.… If our discernment doesn't lead to appropriate action…it's worthless *(NEAH 122).*

8. REAL LIFE: You and a group of friends—including Stephanie, a girl you're attracted to—walk up to a movie theater, undecided about which movie to pick. The consensus suddenly swings toward one that you know will undermine your control over sexual temptation. When you hesitate, Stephanie says, "Come on, it's just a movie…not real life."

   You have twenty minutes before showtime. How will you respond to Stephanie and the others? How can you tactfully guard your own heart, and maybe even help your friends guard theirs?

9. "I will set before my eyes no vile thing." Why? Because I want to know God. I don't want anything to draw my heart away from Him. I want to love holiness (*NEAH* 124).

   Take a moment and talk to God about your love for Him and His love for you. Then brainstorm several steps you might take in order to choose your entertainment more carefully (see *NEAH* 125–127 for ideas).

10. From your ideas in question 9, choose only one or two and transfer them to step 11 in your Custom-Tailored Action Plan on page 70 of this study guide. Ask God for courage and devotion to Him as you face the many small decisions ahead.

    Sometimes we treat entertainment as if it's some kind of right, something essential to our existence. But it isn't. There is no such thing as "must-see TV."… The only thing that's essential is walking with God and pleasing Him. And if that sometimes requires cutting back on what we watch, it's no real sacrifice (*NEAH* 126–127).

ACCOUNTABILITY FOLLOW-UP

11. How have your preventative measures regarding masturbation worked out (see step 10 of your Action Plan)? Do you need to revise your Action Plan? Are you drawing upon God's grace?

12. How close has God been to the center of your heart's affections this last week?

MEDITATE AND MEMORIZE

Test everything.
Hold on to the good.
Avoid every kind of evil.
1 THESSALONIANS 5:21-22

Lone Rangers Are Dead Rangers

Why Is Accountability So Important?

You've learned in *Not Even a Hint* chapter 8 about how critical accountability is for Christians. Good accountability partners may not pop up immediately, but the time and effort spent finding them will ultimately pay off greatly.

Talk now to God about your feelings regarding accountability. Ask Him to guide you to guys who will be effective partners, or ask Him to give your current partners truth, wisdom, and compassion as they hold you accountable.

1. What first comes to your mind when you hear the word *accountability*? How did you develop these impressions?

CENTRAL ISSUES

- The Christian life is something we were designed to do together. Find a good local church, take initiative to get involved, and seek accountability relationships.
- There are several practical guidelines for accountability.

KEY GROWTH OBJECTIVES

✓ To see the importance of strong Christian fellowship.
✓ To learn a few practical dos and don'ts of accountability.
✓ To establish a specific plan of action.

2. Tell about a past experience you've had with accountability. If it was good, tell why. If it was a bad experience, what went wrong?

IS ACCOUNTABILITY FOR ME?

If you cringe at the idea of accountability, it may be because you've never experienced *healthy* accountability. We're in a battle, and we need to watch each other's backs (see *NEAH* 133–136, 138–140).

> Our enemy goes after people who have isolated themselves from other Christians. Stragglers make easy victims. Without other people to encourage them, watch out for them, and confront small compromises in their lives, they often end up drifting into serious sin....
>   We need other Christians to speak, sing, and sometimes shout the truths of God's Word to us. We need others to pray for us when we're in the midst of temptation. We need friends who will hold on to us when we're ready to give up. We need friends who will challenge and even rebuke us when we're indulging in sin (*NEAH* 133–134).

3. According to these Scripture passages, why do we need each other? *Ecclesiastes 4:9–10, 12*

   1 Thessalonians 5:14

   Hebrews 3:12–13

4. The church is at the center of God's plan; it definitely shouldn't be on the outskirts of our lives.... God wants us to be connected to a local church and under the spiritual leadership of pastors and elders. Without this we won't grow (*NEAH* 135).

Even if you're involved in some other Christian group, why is it important to become strongly involved in a local church?
Ephesians 4:11–16

Hebrews 10:24–25

5. Is there anything keeping you from starting an accountability partnership or group? Or keeping you from sharing as honestly as you need to in your current partnership?

THE BEST WAY TO DO IT

6. Of the five "common mistakes" Josh describes in *NEAH* (140–145), which do you think you'll have the hardest time overcoming? Why do you think this is?

7. How can you and your accountability partner(s) plan together for success in overcoming this common mistake? (Do you need to ask God for humility or courage?)

8. **Repentance involves a change of heart and a decision to turn away from a sin. It's proven over time and involves an ongoing choice to put sin to death** (*NEAH* 142).

Give an example of one way you might show genuine repentance, not stopping with confession only.

9. Often, when a person is confessing sin, they're more aware of
   their sinfulness than they are of God's grace and mercy. It's a
   mistake to think that emphasizing guilt will lead to change. The
   opposite is true. It's only when we remember that God has
   forgiven our sin because of Jesus Christ that we can find the
   resolve to keep battling sin (*NEAH* 145).

In what area are you likely to experience "gospel amnesia," forget-
ting God's grace and mercy toward you?

Stop and pray about this, thanking God for forgiving you. Consider
meditating on Psalm 103:8–14.

SETTING UP YOUR ACCOUNTABILITY

10. When you humble yourself and take the step of confessing lust,
    God will give you more grace to battle that very sin (*NEAH* 140).

If you don't already have an accountability partner or group, pray
for God's guidance. Then think of at least one guy around your age or
an older man you would trust. Read back through Josh's suggestions for
selecting partners in *NEAH* (136–138). Write down the names that
come to mind.

11. Start contacting your potential partners right away to explain your
    idea and to invite them to begin meeting with you. When you get
    the number of partners you want (we recommend groups of four or
    fewer), meet as soon as possible and work out the other details of

your accountability relationship. Fill in the details of steps 1–5 in your Custom-Tailored Action Plan (page 68 of this study guide) as you make these decisions.

12. If you already have an accountability partnership or group, complete steps 1–5 in your Custom-Tailored Action Plan. Choose one or two of Josh's suggestions to discuss with your partner or group, looking for ways to sharpen the effective edge of your interaction.

ACCOUNTABILITY FOLLOW-UP

13. How have your plans for carefully selecting your entertainment helped you this week? (See step 11 of your Action Plan.)

14. Can you think of any new ways we can encourage and support you?

MEDITATE AND MEMORIZE

*And let us consider how we may spur one
another on toward love and good deeds.*
HEBREWS 10:24

The Sword of the Spirit

How Can the Truth Help Me Defeat the Lies?

CENTRAL ISSUES

- Reading, meditating on, and memorizing God's Word fills us with life-giving truth that protects us from worldly lies about sex.
- For every lie about sex there is scriptural truth that addresses it.
- Dwelling on God's truth helps us remember that the pleasures of God are far greater than the pleasures of lust.

KEY GROWTH OBJECTIVES

✓ To understand the importance of God's living Word in your daily life.
✓ To apply at least one scriptural truth to a lie you struggle with now.
✓ To establish a specific plan for memorizing and applying God's Word daily.

Now that you've read chapter 9 in *Not Even a Hint,* think about how you're daily surrounded by and flooded with the powerfully alluring lies of the world. While that may seem overwhelming, even greater are the power and pleasure God's Word promises. And God doesn't lie.

Before you start this lesson, ask God to fill you with conviction that His Word is true, living, and powerful and to give you a hunger for Himself and His Word.

1. Tell about a true statement you learned as a child (from the Bible, your parents, a teacher) that has proven helpful in a time of need.

2. What is one reason you might forget you're involved in a life-and-death spiritual battle?

THE POWER OF A PROMISE

Let's look at the importance of God's Word in our lives (see *NEAH* 147–151).

> My goal is to do more than just suggest a few memory verses—I want to help you develop a *conviction* that Scripture is the only weapon that can successfully fight off lust.
>   Can you imagine how foolish it would be for a soldier to go into battle without his weapon or for him to let it fall into disrepair? As Christians, it's just as foolish for us to fight lust without the only offensive weapon God has given us (*NEAH* 150).

3. According to these passages, why is God's Word essential to your daily life?
   Ephesians 6:10–13, 17

   Hebrews 4:12

4. Scripture cuts through the confusion and hazy half-truths that our sin generates. It reveals our wrong desires. It rebukes our apathy. It corrects our selfish human thinking. It unmasks the deception of sin. It points us to God's goodness and faithfulness when we're tempted to forget. It trains us in righteousness. It counters the false promises of lust with God's true promises (*NEAH* 151).

What does God Himself say His Word does for us?
Psalm 119:9–11

Psalm 119:92–93

Psalm 119:104–105

2 Timothy 3:16–17

1 John 2:14

Stop for a moment and think about your attitude toward the Bible. How strongly do you depend on God's Word in your daily life? How much do you hunger for the heart of God, which is revealed in His Word? Talk these questions over with Him, and ask Him to give you an even stronger passion for His Word each day.

CLAIMING THE PROMISE

Now let's practice applying God's Word to a lie you've struggled with recently.

5. Look over the lies Josh lists in *NEAH* (152–157), and think about any other lies you've been tempted by lately. Choose one that you'd like to address, and write it here, using any wording you wish.

LIE of Lust:

6. Stop and ask God for wisdom to deal with this lie. Find a passage of
   Scripture that reveals the lie for what it is, supplying the truth instead.
   You might find it among those Josh has suggested (*NEAH* 152–157),
   or you might find it by using a concordance or a Bible dictionary, or
   by asking someone. When you find it, write it below.

   TRUTH of God's Word:

7. Now take a few minutes to meditate and pray over the passage.
   Several ways to do this are listed. Use whichever ideas are most
   helpful to you.

   • Read the passage aloud several times, emphasizing different words
     or phrases each time. Think about why God chose to word the
     passage this way.
   • Think about the differences between this truth and the lie you've
     written above.
   • If appropriate, insert your name and personalize the passage.
   • Think about the implications of the passage in your life, especially
     as it addresses the lie you've written above.
   • Thank God for making His truth plain instead of leaving you victim
     to lies.
   • Ask God for the power to apply this truth and to resist the lie.
     Request His help with specific actions and decisions.
   • Praise and thank God for the changes He will make in your heart as
     He engraves this truth on it.

By practicing biblical meditation on a Scripture passage, focusing
on its meaning and application, you'll discover that memorization

comes much more easily. Now you're memorizing meaning, not just words. You're relating directly to God, not just to a page in a book.

> **The key to holiness is satisfaction in God—faith that He is more to be desired than anything this world has to offer. We're not just turning away from lust; we're turning toward true satisfaction and joy in God** (*NEAH* 158–159).

LIVING THE PROMISE

8. Go through Josh's list of Scripture passages in *NEAH,* pages 152–157, along with any other passages you might consider hiding in your heart. Choose the first five you want to memorize, and write them under step 14 of your Custom-Tailored Action Plan on page 71 of this study guide. Mark the passage you'll start with.

9. Now think about the best times, places, and methods for your memorization plan. Consider Josh's suggestions in *NEAH,* page 158, as well as the meditation exercise in question 8. Then fill in steps 15–17 of your Action Plan.

ACCOUNTABILITY FOLLOW-UP

10. Have you made progress toward establishing an accountability partnership? Or, if you're already in one, are you making the most of the partnership for your growth and holiness?

11. What about the *other* parts of your Action Plan to date? Is there an area in which you've experienced victory, or one for which you'd like our focused prayer?

MEDITATE AND MEMORIZE

How can a young man keep his way pure?
By living according to your word.
I have hidden your word in my heart
that I might not sin against you.
PSALM 119:9, 11

Holiness Is a Harvest

How Can I Sow to the Spirit?

CENTRAL ISSUES

- The principle of the harvest (Galatians 6:7–9) requires diligence and daily dependence on God's grace.
- Rather than making resistance to sexual temptation our primary preoccupation, we should focus on sowing to the Spirit in order to ensure a harvest of holiness.
- There are several practical ideas for sowing to the Spirit.

KEY GROWTH OBJECTIVES

✓ To recognize the reality of the harvest principle in your life.
✓ To make sowing to the Spirit your priority.
✓ To establish a specific plan for sowing to the Spirit.

Holiness is not defined only by the sin we avoid, but even more by the godliness we pursue. And it doesn't happen overnight. Even though we'd like a quick fix for lust, chapter 10 reminds us that holiness requires consistent, faithful sowing to the Spirit. Take a moment to ask God to give you faith for a lifelong pursuit of holiness. Ask Him to fill you with excitement at His promise of a coming harvest of righteousness.

1. What's an example in our culture (e.g., in the news, a movie, or a commercial) of people denying the law of sowing and reaping? Do you see people acting as though they can escape the consequences of foolish actions and choices?

2. Do you have any important questions related to lust that this study guide has not helped you answer? How might you find help with these questions? (Consider talking to a pastor, a Christian counselor, or some other Christian leader.)

RECOGNIZING THE HARVEST PRINCIPLE

There are two fields before each of us...two kinds of seeds we can plant (see *NEAH* 161–165).

> **What you see in your spiritual life today is the direct result of what you've put in the soil of your life in days past. We can't get around this truth. There are no exceptions—our actions and choices can't be separated from specific consequences** (*NEAH* 163).

3. Read Galatians 6:7–9. List below three small sinful indulgences you're likely to be tempted by in the next few days. Then describe the harvest that comes from such sowing.

Small sinful indulgences   *The harvest (consequences)*

_____   _____

_____   _____

_____   _____

4. **We want to stop sowing seeds to the flesh. But that's not all we should do. Even more, we want to sow seeds in the field of righteousness** (*NEAH* 164).

Now list three small ways you can sow to the Spirit in the next few days, along with the harvest it will produce.

Small ways of sowing to the Spirit	The harvest (spiritual fruit in your life)
_____	_____
_____	_____
_____	_____

5. Now read carefully through Galatians 5:16–25. Summarize the message of this passage in two to four sentences.

CHOOSING HOW TO SOW

As Josh explains in *NEAH* pages 165–170, there are hundreds of ways to sow to the Spirit, but a few habits are especially critical.

> I believe that communing daily with God through reading His Word, through prayer, and through self-examination is among the most essential ways we can sow to the Spirit....
> The greatest privilege of my life isn't writing or speaking or being a pastor—it is relating to, communicating with, and knowing the Creator of the universe.... There is nothing more wonderful! And there's nothing more important in our fight against lust (*NEAH* 166–167).

6. How does each of these passages describe the highest priority and privilege in our lives?
Psalm 27:4, 8

Psalm 73:25–26

John 17:3

Philippians 3:7–14

7. What will it take in your life to make your devotional time with God the number one priority of each day? Do you need to cut back or eliminate some competing activity?

I don't think we should make overcoming lust our primary preoccupation—we need to make the gospel and God's glory our focus. We need to give ourselves to knowing Him, worshiping Him, and meeting with Him every day. The result will be the weakening of lust and a growing passion for godliness (*NEAH* 169–170).

REAPING THE HARVEST FOR LIFE

You will only succeed at making daily time with God your priority if you also make a plan and take it seriously.

8. Describe the best time and place for your daily time with God.

9. How could you use that daily time? Which books of the Bible might you start reading? What might you pray for? What habits of self-examination could you establish?

10. Pray over the ideas you've raised in questions 8 and 9, asking God for wisdom. Then complete steps 12 and 13 in your Custom-Tailored Action Plan. (Remember, you can revise your plan as needed.)

If you have worked through this entire study guide, you should now have a completed Action Plan. We recommend that you make a copy and put it in your Bible or some other safe place. Also give copies to your accountability partners. Review your plan and use it as a guide for daily prayer. Celebrate every small and large victory, and seek God's forgiveness when you lapse.

Don't give up! God has a rich harvest of holiness in store for you (Galatians 6:9). And remember that our hope is in Jesus Christ—in His death and resurrection. Martin Luther summed it up in the words of "A Mighty Fortress Is Our God":

> Did we in our own strength confide,
> Our striving would be losing,
> Were not the right man on our side,
> The man of God's own choosing.
> Dost ask who that may be?
> Christ Jesus, it is He—
> Lord Sabaoth His name,
> From age to age the same,
> And *He* must win the battle.

The right Man is on our side, gentlemen! He has won the battle, and through His power we can obey and glorify Him with our sexuality.

ACCOUNTABILITY FOLLOW-UP

11. Have you started meditating on and memorizing a new Scripture passage this week (or continued work on one)? How is it going? Do you need to revise your Action Plan in any way (see steps 14–17 on page 71)?

12. At this point in your life, how can we most effectively pray for you as you sow to the Spirit?

MEDITATE AND MEMORIZE

> *Do not be deceived: God cannot be mocked.*
> *A man reaps what he sows.*
> *The one who sows to please his sinful nature,*
> *from that nature will reap destruction;*
> *the one who sows to please the Spirit,*
> *from the Spirit will reap eternal life.*
> *Let us not become weary in doing good,*
> *for at the proper time we will reap a harvest if we do not give up.*
> GALATIANS 6:7-9

Custom-Tailored
Action Plan

You will find the guidelines for completing this plan in lessons 4–10 of this study guide.

Keep in mind: This plan is *completely flexible*. It can change as you grow. If a commitment becomes habit and you want to add a new commitment, or if you discover you've set the bar too high or too low on one of your goals, or if you desire to update or adjust part of your plan, *do it*.

This worksheet is designed for easy photocopying for yourself or for your accountability partners.

MY PLAN FOR ACCOUNTABILITY (LESSON 8)

1. Name(s) of my accountability partner(s):

2. When and how often we will communicate:

3. How and where we will communicate (meeting, phone, e-mail):

4. What I want to be asked (simply walking through this completed worksheet is one option):

5. How we will ensure follow-up (so that past commitments won't be forgotten):

MY LUST TRIGGERS (LESSON 4)

Consider making this page a daily prayer list for yourself and your account-ability partner(s).

6. One time of day I'm especially susceptible to temptation:

7. One type of location that presents strong temptation for me:

8. Sources of strong sexual temptation for me (e.g., TV, newspaper, magazines, music, books, Internet, mail—*list no more than three at this time*):

9. From among 6–8 above, the *one* trigger I choose for focused battle now (in God's grace and strength):

DEALING WITH MASTURBATION (LESSON 6)

10. My action step(s) *(no more than two)*:

Don't forget God's forgiveness and power for change (see 1 John 1:9).

DEALING WITH THE MEDIA (LESSON 7)

11. My action step(s) *(no more than two)*:

SOWING TO THE SPIRIT (LESSON 10)

12. The time and place for my daily devotional time with God.

13. What I will do during that time (where in Scripture I'll read, what I'll pray for, how I'll examine myself):

GOD'S TRUTH TO ANSWER THE WORLD'S LIES (LESSON 9)

14. Five Scripture passages for my meditation and memorization (*add more as needed*):

15. How I will do my meditation and memorization:

16. When and how often:

17. Where:

HELPING MY FEMALE FRIENDS AVOID SEXUAL TEMPTATION (LESSON 5)

18. My action step(s) (*no more than two*):

Purity Download

Seven Tips for Fighting Internet Porn

BY JOSHUA HARRIS

The Internet is a wonderful tool. We can use it to work, to study, even to share the gospel with people in other parts of the world. But if we're not careful it can become a door to great sin and spiritual ruin. Many Christian men, even leaders and pastors, have fallen prey to the temptation of Internet pornography. It's instantly accessible and easily hidden from others. But God sees all our sin. And Internet porn will always lead to heartache and regret. Whether or not this is a current area of temptation for you, the following seven tips will equip you to honor God on-line.

1. IDENTIFY WHAT'S LEADING UP TO LUSTFUL INDULGENCE ON THE INTERNET.

For many guys, sin on-line is preceded by compromise in areas such as their fantasies, television viewing, or reading material. It might seem like sexual sin on-line "comes out of nowhere," but it's really something guys build up to through disobedience in other areas. Prayerfully consider where you can be fighting these little battles more diligently.

2. RESOLVE THAT NO TECHNOLOGICAL CONVENIENCE IS WORTH SINNING AGAINST GOD.

Most people have to use the Internet for school or work. But we should never place the convenience of technology above God's commands for holiness. If you've struggled with Internet porn, be willing to take radical action. Maybe that means no Internet access at your home for a season. Or not having high-speed access. It could mean going on-line only when you're with other people. My dad has only one computer in his house with a web browser, and that computer is in the middle of the living room. But that's not all...my mom is the only one with the password to get onto it! Inconvenient? Incredibly so! But he's more concerned with protecting himself and my younger brothers than with convenience.

3. Examine your mind-set when browsing and the amount of time spent on-line.

If Internet use has become a mindless entertainment activity, where your brain goes into neutral, you're in dangerous territory. You might not be struggling with Internet porn right now, but there's a good chance that this mind-set will lead to compromise. Go on-line with a purpose. And don't spend tons of time browsing aimlessly. Cutting back so that the time you spend on-line is focused and has a point will significantly cut back on the temptation to slip into the darker corners of the Web.

4. Have an accountability partner that consistently asks about your Internet activity.

Even if you don't have a history of struggling with Internet porn, we should all have a friend who regularly asks how we're doing in this area. Find someone and get him to commit to bringing up the subject consistently.

5. Make your definition of "over the line" far from the edge of the cliff.

Jared has been struggling with temptation to look at on-line porn for a week. He's been stretching his resolve by visiting somewhat questionable sites and the urge to indulge is growing. Unfortunately, he doesn't share this with his accountability partner. Instead he battles in secret. But a week later he "really messes up" and spends two hours browsing porn sites. Do you see the problem? Jared's definition of "over the line" when it comes to sin is right at the edge of the cliff—when he finally confesses he's already fallen.

When it comes to accountability, I think it's important to back up our definition of blowing it on-line. We need to involve others much earlier in the process of temptation. So confess when you're dabbling with somewhat questionable sites (or okay sites with provocative ads). Share when you're spending too much time on-line. Make these things your definition of messing up so your friends can pray for you and challenge you long before you slip off the edge of temptation. Thomas Watson once wrote, "A godly man will not go as far as he may, lest he go further than he should."

6. Use website filters, blockers, and accountability software as a final line of defense, not the first.

Programs that e-mail a list of all the websites you visit or block bad content are a wonderful tool. But they can't replace a heart that truly hates sin and desires to please God. Utilize them *after* you've taken a look at your heart and examined the lies you tell yourself in the process of temptation. Do the work of digging into God's Word, meditating on Scripture, making yourself accountable, and other steps listed above. Blocking and accountability software can then serve to support your heart convictions instead of trying to substitute them.

7. Fight this sin the hardest when you're feeling strong.

Many guys experience a level of "victory" over Internet porn for a season—only to be lulled into a false sense of security and fall again. If you're experiencing a time of relative freedom from the sin of Internet pornography, that's good...but don't stop watching this part of your life carefully. It's when you're feeling strong that you should fight the hardest. In other words, kick sin when it's down. You don't have to fight like a gentleman here. Redouble your grace-motivated efforts. Keep "backing up" your definition of on-line compromise. Memorize Scripture. Pray for God's power. By doing so you'll weaken the power of this sin in your life even more.

Joshua Harris is a pastor at Covenant Life, a thriving church in a Maryland suburb of Washington, D.C.

Joshua got his start in writing as the editor of *New Attitude,* a Christian magazine for homeschool teens. He wrote his first book, *I Kissed Dating Goodbye,* at age twenty-one and that same year moved from Oregon to Gaithersburg, Maryland, to be trained for pastoral ministry under C. J. Mahaney. Five years after giving up the dating game himself, he met, courted, and married his bride, Shannon. He shares their love story and the lessons God taught them in his second book, *Boy Meets Girl: Say Hello to Courtship.*

Joshua and Shannon now have two children, Emma Grace and Joshua Quinn. For information about Josh's work, visit:

www.joshharris.com
www.covlife.org

Feel free to contact Josh. Though he can't respond personally to all correspondence, he'd love to get your feedback.

Joshua Harris
P.O. Box 249
Gaithersburg, MD 20884-0249
DOIT4JESUS@aol.com

Not Just for Men

SHANNON & JOSHUA HARRIS

WITH BRIAN SMITH

A STUDY GUIDE FOR WOMEN

not *even* a hint

Lust isn't just a guy problem—it's a human problem. This biblical study companion to Joshua Harris's powerful bestselling book is designed specifically for women, for use at home or in small groups.

ISBN 1-59052-354-7

Tired of the game?
Kiss dating goodbye.

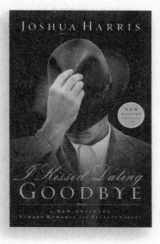

I KISSED DATING GOODBYE

Dating. Isn't there a better way? Reorder your romantic life in the light of God's Word and find more fulfillment than the dating game could ever give—a life of purposeful singleness.

ISBN 1-59052-135-8

I KISSED DATING GOODBYE VIDEO SERIES

Three-video series   ISBN 1-59052-180-3
Video-Part 1: Love   ISBN 1-59052-212-5
Video-Part 2: Purity   ISBN 1-59052-213-3
Video-Part 3: Trust   ISBN 1-59052-214-1

I KISSED DATING GOODBYE STUDY GUIDE

The *I Kissed Dating Goodbye Study Guide*, based on Joshua Harris's phenomenal bestseller provides youth with a new resource for living a lifestyle of sincere love, true purity, and purposeful singleness.

ISBN 1-59052-136-6

Say Hello to Courtship

This dynamic sequel picks up where *I Kissed Dating Goodbye* left off. Joshua and Shannon Harris share their inspiring experience of how a joyous alternative to recreational dating—biblical courtship—worked for them. *Boy Meets Girls* helps couples journey from friendship to marriage while avoiding the pitfalls of today's often directionless relationships. It gives practical advice about communication, involving your family in your relationship, keeping your relationship pure, dealing with past sexual sin, and the questions to ask before you get engaged.

ISBN 1-57673-709-8